The Radio Tree

Corey Marks

New Issues Poetry & Prose

A Green Rose Book

New Issues Poetry & Prose
The College of Arts and Sciences
Western Michigan University
Kalamazoo, Michigan 49008

First Edition, 2012.

ISBN: 978-1-936970-06-3 (paperbound)

Library of Congress Cataloging-in-Publication Data:
Marks, Corey
The Radio Tree/Corey Marks
Library of Congress Control Number: 2011943421

Editor:	William Olsen
Guest Editor:	Nancy Eimers
Managing Editor:	Kimberly Kolbe
Layout Editor:	Elizabyth A. Hiscox
Assitant Editor:	Traci Brimhall
Art Director:	Ern Bernhardi
Designer:	Meredith Felt
Production:	Paul Sizer
	The Design Center, Frostic School of Art
	College of Fine Arts
	Western Michigan University
Printing:	McNaughton & Gunn, Inc.

The Radio Tree

~~Corey Marks~~   3/28/13

For MacKenzie,

What a pleasure
chatting with you about
poetry today — & welcome
to Texas. Best of luck
with your poems.

New Issues

WESTERN MICHIGAN UNIVERSITY

Also by Corey Marks

Renunciation

For Madeleine

Contents

The Radio Tree

All night she walked until she came to a forest
and in the forest a hollow tree split like two waves.
A radio yammered from inside: her mother's
voice—not as it is now, but as it was once—
and then her father's, answering, though what
and for what reason she couldn't catch, the way
at times in the backseat she would hear them
speaking less in words than strings of sound
that tied and untied and unraveled into silences
while she looked out the window at the long
black wires stretched pole by pole into the open
distance that carried other voices she couldn't hear
and where birds settled in ones and twos to make
their own declarations lost to her in the whir
of the car gliding over gray rural roads. So many
things not speaking to her across such distances.
She would look through the near world
pouring past to the far points that remained
almost steady. They'd pleased her, those moments,
with a loneliness she knew was her own,
but she would listen differently now,
wouldn't she, knowing what she knows.
The radio's round face glowed inside the tree.
She turned a dial. Static rushed sentences
stripped of words and still strange to her,
estranged, as though she remained a child.
But these voices weren't her childhood,
they were that other world of her parents' lives.
A bare wire sparking elsewhere in the rain.
A thrush scuttling into a clear cut's far bracket.
She thought of how, once, she woke in the night,
walked out of her house across one road,
then another and into the damaged fields, walked
until she came to a forest she'd never seen. Tidy
black rows of trees arranged there by someone's
need for order. A second growth. Then an opening
in the dark like two waves lit from within.

Three Bridges

When the rains came I was, for my own purposes,
on the far side of the river. Who could've known
the drizzle would ratchet to torrent, or the river
unbuckle, swallow its banks, ring the scattered trees

like so many necks trying to stay afloat, strip boats
from their moorings and batter them out of the river's throat
into the mouths of other rivers? Or that it would wash out

the town's three bridges: the one too narrow to walk
two abreast, the one beyond the last houses, already ruined,
abandoned by all but reckless boys and swallows,

even the one, story goes, someone made a pact
with the devil to build, the one I crossed in the morning
as it arched in the uneasy air like a wing.

And by the time I had to leave what I'd come to do
half-done, the rain made it hard to see, coming down
and never done with falling. Everything bleared,

went pale and indistinct. My clothes weighed
as much as a child. I fell, and the rain struck me
clean. I lost my way and found a river I didn't recognize

in its frenzy, whitecaps shearing its surface like teeth.
Even when the rains died, the flood kept on, worrying
the absent bridges, the water thick with silt, its current
full of animals coiled in the rush. I couldn't dare it.

Where's the devil when his deal falls through
its own reflection? Now the bridge is half of what it was,
reversed in the river bottom leading nowhere

I want to go. At least from here I can see my house,
my daughter when she walks into the yard with a pail.
She looks up by chance, and though she must wonder

what's become of me, she doesn't see my waving arm,
an unrecognizable motion in a landscape she knows
she should know but doesn't anymore. Or she sees me
in too many places to keep track; I'm the one missing

thing missing everywhere. But then her eyes catch
on the swallows sweeping the bloated river—no way
back to their roosts now, they lift away to take an eyeful
of everything that isn't what it was. And move on . . .

This must be what death is like: those left behind
look up sometimes where they think you should be,
but if they see you at all it's from too far to make sense

of what you've become—a color bled briefly
into sight through a whirl of silt. And then—who can
blame them, there's so much to do to reclaim the house,
to live in it again—they look away, and you're left

waiting for the river to settle back between the banks
that held it in place all your life and become itself again.

A Brief Account of My Thirty-Third Year

My Jesus year. Everyone who makes it
this far has one, my father said.

Even those who don't believe,
like my father in 1964, too old already

for all the dying to come. And my year?
We cleaned the high windows

at the lake house. The year a new war
refused its scripted end. Year we hated

the president all the more. Year of drought,
pines like tinder, fire a tongue barely held

back from what it most wanted to say.
Year a student yelled at me for how

the words I made her read damaged her soul.
Year I didn't believe in her soul.

Year the clouds promised themselves
across the felt-board sky, but came

to nothing, like so many new treatments
for the same disease. Pills and needles. No rain.

Year the migrations paused to drink our bowls
dry; a tally of colors in the scorched air.

Year my daughter learned to walk
and pretend to cry. Then

Ontario was burning. Smoke bled
across the lake, someone else's loss

come to remind us of our own.
Year wasps entered the small windows

of the lantern along the path:
a papery comb distended

from the roof like another lantern.
A hard light to see clearly by,

so I put my ear to the open windows
to hear a new way of saying

the old things: *fire* and *grief*,
but no word for consolation.

Year a score of finches broke their necks
believing only what they could see.

Year I flew at my own windows. Year
I didn't think my father could die.

Dumb Luck

The horse—her number smudged
by sweat and thumbs nuzzling

predictable exactas
stamped in black—stumbles

at the last, run too hard, run
beyond what her ankles could bear,

and the jockey, who'd driven
her ahead of the other horses

now churning past and flinging
back rings of dust, rides

her down, out of the grace
and rush of the race and into the hoof-

torn dirt, the shit and grit
and the shudder he's lost control of . . .

Then another rush: people
flurry to the fallen animal, the jockey

is raised, stunned and still
he feels he's moving—something roils

in him, around him, under him.
Words are inconsequential

as flies. Dumb luck.
The animal won't rise.

Nearby, the winner paces,
cooling, saddled now with the reason

for the day, heavy chest
widening against his rider's approval,

each breath ragged and expendable
and replaceable as the printed bets

that drift the grounds, skittering
between knuckles of grass

beneath the stands where people
stare, the ones who got it wrong,

used to seeing what doesn't come,
to wagering chances bound to be

nothing, nothing, nothing
but lost. Though someone got it right

and smacks his ticket
against his palm, exactly sure

of what it bears. He looks away
as the crowd around him cranes

and gawks into the afterlife
of chance—a white truck,

a man with an open-mouthed kit.
A needle. The hurtling world

closes like a gate.

Loss

Comes like a knee to the back
        and a mouthful of questions. I close

the door, walk away from the houses clenched
        inside the shoreline's jaw, past

the snow-hulled boats pitched above ground

        to where the lake beats its pillars of ice,
a broken city blue and fluming at the opening

        of the bay. Wind ruffles at my face
like a hand that means to be

        more gentle than it knows how.

At the blue edges, ice piles in slabs,
        rises in funnels, peaks and trenches,

splits fractures large enough for a body
        to slip through. Water rasps

beneath me, urgent as breath—
        this isn't where the dead go.

        Here, small holes open like sleeves
lined with blue—I slide my arm

        into one as though trying on a coat
to wear the long and foreign season,

        but I can't fill it with my reach.
Beneath my knees the ice cricks and scrapes

        its bruised answers to the ravening water.
Ask again, Father, there's nothing

        I wouldn't tell you now.

Heirlooms

The table isn't set for the son with its two forks
at each place, its dull and sharp knives.
Fists of bread wait to open, but not in his hands.
A bowl of late apples is another matter,
so overfilled it would be easy to filch one
while the voices in the kitchen worry at his arrival.
How couldn't they keep him in mind,
the man and woman whispering together
like one thing sharpening another?

Couldn't they imagine that though he'd left,
he'd knock on the door one evening
late in the year, the orchards beyond the yard
bent and spilling their last windfall? The photos
are missing, the ones he would point to
if he could. Replaced with trinkets, lovely
and small and nothing to do with him.
How completely he's gone from this place—
nothing will look at him, nothing

will meet his eye. Even the mouse
keeps to its hole behind the hutch.
Above the table, windows square themselves
with the night, giving over to reflection,
to how he's seated in the middle chair
as though he'd never grown large and unchildlike
and unrecognizable. He looks to himself
like what he's always been becoming.
Beyond, the yard darkens, blanker

and blanker, unblemished, until only a tree
flinches behind his face, skittery as thought.
Or some animal testing the yard, taking
ignorance for a kind of welcome. The guests
have their own arrivals in mind as they drive
the familiar stretches between houses.
They think they know the house they'll enter.
Its conversations. The claims it makes.
The rich smell of blood darkening in a pan.

In the kitchen, the voices are fine-boned now,
delicate as wrists turned up. Soon
one of them will step through the doorway
with an answer. Angry or not. Wounded
or not. The son has no explanation
for his time away. His silence. It was easier
for a while to say nothing, to assume
he'd been forgotten. He should leave.
He meant nothing by coming here.

Or meant something no longer expected.
In the meantime, he's stolen an apple—
sharp, sweet fleshed and not, he knows,
for him. Still, he loves the sound of his teeth
popping through the red, wrist-thin skin.
One of the old varieties, Winesap
or Smokehouse. Nonesuch. Heirlooms,
names for tastes he'd nearly forgotten
he wanted to taste again. And the same poison

speckled across the skin clings to his tongue
like sleep, as though he's waking at last
from a dream in which he knew himself
to find an empty table, his face in a window
blinded and burned out by headlights,
one pair then another, and strangers
gathering now from the dark, laughing and
looking up toward the house they know
will welcome them as they imagined it would.

The String

unspools someone's
carelessness

out of the sun-
bleached day

toward a culvert's
dark underside

where it threads
a broken bottle's

teeth, tangles twigs
and leaves and trash

into a reckoning
of what we can

do without—partial,
but the string goes on

with its work,
its daily, studious

accumulations
strung along knot

by knot, a time-
line forgotten

with the ease of
a hand letting go.

Though here's a child
who comes to trace

the string's trail
down the slope

and under the wind-
scoured overpass

she's been told never
to hide beneath

in a storm, who
pinches her small

hand into a loop
she slides over

snarls, burrs, a straw
sleeve, tentacles

of magnetic
tape, a cluster

of fur, the string
she thinks of as

a tornado
she's unraveled

to see what's inside
all that gathering;

there is so much
she doesn't want

to forget: crickets
scattering before

her into darkness,
the dry cough of her

shoes on cement,
cars clattering

over her head
like storm clouds

oblivious
to the thrill

of something new
unraveling

from a forgotten
length of string.

The Empty Theater

I woke to the sound of teeth grinding
in someone else's mouth. I was alone.

When the noise came again, it was a door
clearing its throat with nothing,

at last, to say. *Branches raking the house,*
I answered in my best version of your voice.

Then the sound became branches
lashing a body as it pushed through a thicket,

dragging at its skin. I sat up, coaxed
into the dark, animal urged.

Who will touch me now? I asked
the empty theater—the rumpled pillows,

the coverlet kicked-aside, our places
so clearly marked we could begin again.

And then it was gone. I ran outside
below trees black against the black sky,

and listened the way a tongue probes
a missing tooth. The anesthesia

of ordinary night-noise spilled
through the yard. I couldn't speak.

I couldn't feel my mouth. The trees
reeled darkly in impenetrable waves.

And Winter

Au Sable Point Lighthouse, Lake Superior, 1879

1.

When Father opens the door, the storm
is with him, it rushes the dark rooms, flushes
dust from the backs of books and unused chairs.
Down the shore a ship has run aground;
Father's seen it from the tower, a row of lanterns
threading toward us through the rain.
                              Ready yourself,
he calls, *light the rooms* . . . The gale raves
over his words with its two mouths—wind
and water. Beyond him, the lake rends
its new scars.
              No home now but this,
Father said in the summer calm
when we arrived, though this is no home.
It is a cage set in the wind.

2.

We have our tasks. Father shrinks into the black
frame of the storm, below the beam
from the hive-shaped lens flailing
the exaggerated night. What choice do we have?
The shipwrecked read a promise in our light
we do not mean.
              I thought we'd taken residence
at the heart of a refusal that sends the coming world away.
Isn't *that* the vocation he chose for us? Carry the oil
up the narrowing spiral, fill the lamp,
wipe the lens, trim the wick,
set blazing its obstinate *No?*

Autumn arrives with its own commandments.
And winter, which won't stay away—isn't
that the arrival the storm prepares? The edges
seize and the bays close hard
and there is no need to tell anyone not to come
where promise shuts
                    its sky-dark door.

Semper Augustus

Broken tulip, seventeenth-century Holland

The plain white petal between her finger and thumb
belled into a sail pregnant with nothing it could bear,
then split, dark seamed, its length. A whole fleet

foundered in the field around her: bands of white tulips,
red and yellow, diluted to shadow beneath
a setting moon splinted against the sky. Each spring,

they lost themselves, kiltered together, no longer
petal and flower but color and field that flared
in daylight and drew inward at night like shutters
no one looked out of. What shame to always wake

to the same thing, she thought. Elsewhere, tulips
turned wily, shot through with someone else's fortune,
but not here, not under her watch. Here,
nothing rivered or flamed, nothing streaked

wildly the way the horses, startled from the stable
last winter, shocked the field with their frantic darks,
giving up the names she and her husband called
as they ran for the canal and the year's first loss.

Once, she'd seen the famed Semper Augustus,
single white flower feathered with red, saw
how it moved, ravenous, starving for the eye.

Even now she closed her eyes and saw the petals,
veined, corrupt—how they sickened her to look at them,
they were that beautiful. She'd even dreamed

the flower stricken by illness, its bulb split
into handfuls hollowing themselves into each late
and later flourish and reflected in a bank of mirrors

meant to multiply the owner's fortune.
Semper Augustus, he'd named it,
and kept its generations mostly to himself,

but in her dream any reason to look disappeared
into wasted husks, and the mirrors froze over,
cracked piecemeal by the seasons into shard
and glint until nothing was left to show.

She'd awakened to a blear of color caught
from her window same as every morning,
spring after spring. How could the flowers in the field

not be the sick ones?—or the sickness itself, spread
as they were like an irritation. And when she knew
she'd lost the child, the name she'd meant for it
a husk on the tongue she couldn't quite swallow back,

she wanted something in the field to draw her eye,
its *now* erupted petal by petal so each flower
demanded its own attention, its intricate hour.
Better to be sick with beauty than despair.

She imagined she could wait for color to craze
the petals, feathering toward her outstretched hand,
imagined her husband at the window behind her,
watching what by will alone she'd drawn from the field.

But the tulips raised the same blank refusal
to rupture, to river and flame, to roil two bodies
into one. Want cannot give what won't come
even to its own name. She thought of how she'd run

through the field in winter, casting her voice
like rope at what wouldn't be saved:
ice splintered and yawed under one horse

crossing the canal; the other bloodied itself
going down, bloodied the ice veined like a widened eye,
the first horse looking back from the other side.

Sleeper Lake Fire

A tree was burning in my dream.
When I woke, a whole forest burned,
though only smoke shouldered
through the near woods. In the dream,

the tree quavered with birds
clustered above flames climbing
the bark. Off-white birds, what kind
I couldn't tell you. Some things drift

from a dream, though when I startled
to smoke skulking through
the house, part of me still heard
the tree, its earful of panic.

Paper torn into chatter. Wings
like little doors popping open.
But I wanted to listen
to the house blue with smoke,

and the window's open mouth.
Something was catching up with us.
A *wildfire*, the radio repeated
in its obvious way, same story

for days. The wind had always
blown another way. Winds
turn. Proverbial. Flames burn
what they can—here, jack pines

and scrub: one tree, then others,
junk pines good only for paper
and fire, all primed to give up
their gangly, fast-grown limbs.

Succession. Yesterday, I broke char
from a stump scorched to a socket
how long ago in the backwoods
of another century I couldn't say.

I gave it to my daughter to draw
a sun and a house and dark birds.
A black tree and a black lake.
She taped her picture on her wall

and called it *Sleeper Lake*
after the new name the radio mutters
these days, after the body of water
curled in on itself like a sleeping child

as the helicopters pass over,
dangling the orange blisters
they mean to spill onto what
they can't put out. When fire

took the low branches,
the birds flurried higher
but wouldn't fly, wouldn't trust
the sky with its smoke-chalked sun.

They crowded boughs tilting
back toward flames open as palms,
but I was elsewhere, already
halfway outside the dream.

The radio warned us to pack,
to bring our photos to the door,
our living and dead. The time
might come, untangling

through the jack pines and scrub
from the lakeside dry as felt
where the sleeper turned
in her narrow shores.

When my daughter wanted a song
before sleep, the radio wouldn't sing.
When she wanted to flush a fear
that wouldn't leave its perch, she asked,

Will you wake me when the fire comes?
Her drawing fluttered above her head,
a present or future or illegible past
lifting from the wall like a wing—

Once there was no house.
Once there was no bed
and no child to sleep in it.
No window left open all night.

Once another tree burned and birds
startled at the sudden blaze,
handfuls of ruckus thrashing
into a night torn between the sky

and the dark page lapping below
where the fire doubled
and grew wilder like a dream
of itself coming true.

Lullaby

I should be used to it by now, the way sparrows rill
to warning as they scatter from the tree across the street
where, third time this week, she trespasses,
scuttling through the lacework again, upward

among hollows close stitched to the pecan's heavy trunk,
branches swayed and rustling as though she's wind
passing through, or breath stirring deep in the body,
some small thing restless in its cage,

this woman who steadied herself on a cane
crossing the field below, stooped in her paces,
each new step needing the training of her eyes.

Each morning she's come, you've slept—
the way, I suppose, the newly recovered must—
in some pointless arrangement between bedclothes
and a body that lost track of what you trust your body to do.

For me, sleep's out the window, restless
as the petty rounds the sparrows cheep, their accounts
of stir and settle. Even the familiar disturbance startles me—
this time from the open page in *Birds of Europe*

and the song I wanted to hear that's always out of earshot.
The little block of prose roosting in my lap says
the singer refuses captivity, dies in its cage;

even to render the sketch the guide offers as measure,
someone broke a bird's neck and pierced its throat with wire
to bend the head into the posture of song,

the throe of a single, silent note that doesn't end.

*

Stir and settle: first their astonished calls, their quick-
flung bodies flushed into flight, and then

it's out of them, beyond them, panic descending
into that other register of calm, the woman in the tree
merely a part of the tree they settle back into, familiar
and wholly within their grasp. I wish you could see her—

though not enough to wake you—wish you could watch
the deft climb I described so poorly last night. Still,
in answer you read from the hardbound *Grimm's*

someone else read to you as a child curled in your bed,
one hand unfurled toward the broken-backed book
cupped in your mother's wider hand;

then, time came all the varied dangers lulled you
to sleep, the book set by, closed on the last sentence heard,
the last child lost, changed, preserved.

Once the book fell to the floor and splayed there,
bird with its song wrung out, I imagined I *could've* followed—
isn't that what the lover always does?—,

that in those days when you were farthest from me
I could find you, even where the hospital's florescence
lit your disheveled bed into an expanse
I hadn't known how to cross, every new thing

gone wrong with your body clear on the distance
of your half-turned face. I imagined I knew
what I didn't then, and led you back
through the briar thicketed between us:

Once, you woke rewritten with a fairytale's logic—
prick your finger and you'll bleed your body out.

*

Last night's story's stuck in the morning's craw:

> *Deep in a wood a girl found one tree so beautiful*
> *she couldn't help but touch it, even though*
> *it wasn't hers to touch. The tree belonged*

to the old woman, feathered as an owl, waiting
in its branches. To teach a lesson, the old woman
changed the girl into a nightingale, placed her

in a cage in a room filled with other cages,
with other nightingales who never wanted to take up
worthless song but had, they learned, no other choice.

All night full throated complaint, but who listened?
Not the old woman asleep in her chair
dreaming of the next day's watch. Not the lover

who found the cottage after weeks of searching,
stood outside its window but couldn't tell
one song from another, couldn't recognize

his beloved's voice, couldn't guess the words
to her lament. The song was a distraction, a bramble,
O how it throttled him, snapped in his face, stung him

away from his purpose. Shut up. *But the birds*
wouldn't stop—Don't you know who I am?
Don't you know, don't you know?

When he found the door he would open each cage
and wring the piercing notes from every last throat.
What did he know of how the body can change?

*

But the story ends too soon, won't give up what
I want of it: what of the bodies raveled below their cages

and the old woman waking not to song but to wind
sucking at the little open doors? *Wait, wait,* what
of the lover wandered back into the forest—does he

know by now? And how do the sparrows soothe their panicked
away, away to *return, return?* How can the woman
unlace her frailty and step so cleanly out of it?

Pay attention, the world demands, but something
always stutters and blurs, and anyway I can never
get enough of what I've already gotten wrong,

what I didn't quite see, or saw, too late, the first time.
When you showed me the first speckle on your forehead,
the trio burst minutely on your cheek, I leaned close,

brushed the spots flush against your skin
and told you not to worry. *Wait and see. A rash,*
something small and already fading. A little tale
we wanted to believe, but hadn't come to the end of

by far; *this* story wanted to keep going. Your body
unstitched our trust in it, thread by thread, pocking
itself with blood that no longer knew to contain itself,

capillaries split and spilt across your face and hands
into a map of a country you'd never thought to visit.

And when I came after you, followed you
to where your body was filled with other bodies' blood,
what could I do but watch? What was I but distraction?

                                        *

Outside, the woman leans easily against the trunk
while her cane rests below, ready to bear her back
out of whatever new surety she's found in the high limbs.

Between her clasped hands she presses two pecans
until they split. When she cracks her small mouth wide
I think for a moment she's breaking into song.

The Black Bear at Closing

The bear presses her shoulder to the glass
of her enclosure in the bluing light
and looks into her habitat, the rutted path,

the cement-bowl pond rimmed with muck,
the red ball lolled against a log—
a creature done with being gawked.

You knock the glass. A primal indifference
twitches her matted back. Elsewhere,
the exhibits clear, children trail the trauma

of their voices through the turnstiles
as evening wallows in their wake.
Some garish bird clocks out the day.

The bear slouches in shadow, ridiculous
and vaguely human, and you lean closer,
nothing more than attention's ghost.

One paw fidgets idly at her knee.
The bears you came to see as a child
must be dead. Not the ones in books

you read, though, that were never alive—
they'd come back if you wanted them. The dead
stay dead. You peer at your own hands,

how they fold and pucker into mouths. *Kiss off,*
the little lips tell each other, toothless
and cruel. Above, loudspeakers announce

what they always announce at this hour.
It hasn't occurred to the guard that you'll be here,
pressed to your own side of the glass,

inches from the bear drawn into herself
as though you're not here, her black fur splayed
against the same transparency resisting your touch.

Wait long enough and curiosity becomes trespass,
like watching a woman in a restaurant
nudge the blunt nub of her nipple

into an infant's mouth to quell an inconsolable
anger. See how the black bear stares
into her paw upturned now in the sprawl of her lap

with the preoccupation of a reader.
Your mother used to read with that intensity—
it bristled a thicket around her. *Mother,*

Mother! Some other voice had her ear,
calling her another direction, into wilderness.
No trail you knew led there. She held

her grief the same way, paged through
as though the loss was a story
she wandered into child-like and alone.

The empty bowl was for her, the broken chair—
remnants to be claimed, sorted, dog-eared.
You left her there. The door closed

like an opening book when you went outside
to skirt the edge of a woods and thrash
the understory with a broken stick.

The Lake

They cannot look out far.
They cannot look in deep.
But when was that ever a bar
To any watch they keep?
—Robert Frost

Deceptive, this calm, the way slow-toppling
waves sooth the shore, smooth it, set it right.
Farther out, the long horizon frays,
a distant disordering between—I want to say sky
and *sea*, but no, it's a lake, immense

landlocked, hemmed in, no salt
to sting the eyes, or bear a body up . . .
A wild place promised, but *we're*
here, all of us, plodding our attentions
along the lake's edge. We came, singly,

to search the stones, wade ankle-
deep in the chill, to taunt the gulls
pivoting from tree-top to fanning wave.
We came to look for whatever we
look for in such places, for the lake's

particular take on blankness, recurrence,
eternity, etc. But not for the swimmer.
He must've seen something in the lake
we couldn't, watching from the warmth
of his car parked between other cars

in the gravel lot. Perhaps he listened
to the lake's dull thrashing beyond the trees
and saw it in shards, something in want
of repair, saw a correspondence there,
an idea he could give himself over to.

The rest of us wouldn't have said a word
to each other, I'm sure of it, wouldn't
have met each other's eyes,
hoisting our field guides just so
we blanked one another from sight,

but then I spied him, churning
past the last sandbar's pale demarcation,
and called out, finger prodding the air
so everyone would mark the body shrinking
by arm-lengths into the shifting blue.

This was no idle swim. At my feet
the little waves performed their pratfalls,
their look-at-me's lolling openmouthed,
but I wouldn't have it, none us of would, we
were all for the swimmer now,

flaying himself into the distant waves
like a penitent. Isn't that how it looked—
like punishment? Persistence?
Something more than we asked
of ourselves? And we didn't ask for this:

to be stolen from our purposes, pieced
into a shared attention. Now the cold
action of the waves shows one thing
and palms another. We can't watch
the turning of its hands closely enough

as though we want more from the swimmer
than he wants from his own body
needling each coming swell
until he becomes our point, stitching us
single-mindedly into the fray.

Bell

The chirr and squabble of birds all morning
and wind coaxing waves to shore outside
the father's bedside window

all joined lately by a distant bell clamoring
for its own clear patch of air swept clean enough
to set up house. The bell

slips below the window's raised lip
like news the son doesn't want to hear

when he comes with a bottle of iodine,
a folded cloth, a roll of gauze.

He could ignore it the way, as a child,
he ignored the bell his father would strike:

cast iron, black, bolted above the door;
it clanged in sets of three, flocks of sound
skimming long corn rows brown

before thrashing and fingered through with shadows
where the son played at being lost.

Come home, it said, *come home, come home,*
but he learned to hold his place, finger

to a page, poor scraps of woodland
and field ringing through his head like a word,
an answer, first knell of something

he couldn't quite fit through the eyehole of his mouth.

He clears the dressing from the surgeon's mark,
peels it gently from stitches strained on skin.

The dull clang through the half-open pane
sounds now like the bell in a story his father read to him
as a child. No one had heard the bell for how long

until an arrow plunked its vine-choked iron.
The hunter, still damning the pheasant flown free,
turned back to what he did strike, quiet now

beneath the leaves. Black bell rusted red.
And when he entered the door beneath the bell
he found in the shallow nave of a stone church

a congregation of skeletons, heads thrown
back as if in song, a hymn of want, mouths opened
like the open mouths of a nest. *A sickness,*

the father explained, *it struck them dead.*

And now the bell cannot say what it meant to say—
fainter, washed over, bickered out of earshot—

and the son can't *stop* listening for it,
the same way he bends close to each whisper
he still doesn't catch. The father's tongue moves

as it used to, against the palate, against the teeth,
its little room, its half-open window.
The son doesn't know how to answer.

Hush, he says at last, agreeing with the wind,
and presses a stained cloth to his father's throat

to clean the wound and let it heal.

Hotel Fire

The alarm, the clamber from sleep, dreams
snapped away like branches in a thicket,
then the doors, all the doors opening,
spilling out their versions of panic,

many-armed in the inconsolable jangle.
And in the midst of it, more frenzied
than most, a worrier, already burned
down to a cluster of explosions.

Someone—she doesn't recall a face, but
a pressure—led her through the stairwell,
out to the parking lot, left her beneath
the security lights, one more of the various

states of distress and undress looking up
to the windows for a flicker of something
more than a few TV's still playing
canned laughter to an audience of empty rooms.

Then a face wafted into one window's
black and blue, three stories up, staring
down. Someone left behind—*No getting out now*—
though still no smoke or fire fanned

behind the steady face, milky, plastic . . .
She pauses, says how she thought then
of the mask that held her husband's head in place
session after session those months

radiation traced its match-point into his neck.
*All this practice holding still—it's like modeling
for a death mask*, he'd joked. *Relax*,
the tech answered, fastening the straps

behind his head. But how could he
relax into the stillness required,
how could he lower his face to the task
with all his concentration focused

the way a carp tests the frozen surface
of the winter pond? How could he
make a *joke* of it? How could he make
her think such a thing? And how could anyone

save the face risen to the window now?
She worried about smoke roiling under
the door, over the bed, the heat, dust and ash,
the coughing fit that wouldn't unclench,

doubling the body like laughter, but not
funny, nothing funny about it, worried
one more of the many deaths to die
before anyone dies, pored over like scales

she never meant to practice . . . *But what happened?*
you insist, impatient as any son.
But you know this one already: the mask
in the window raised a hand, pale blue

and waving. Someone laughed, someone
shouted. The siren died. And in her chest,
blood trundled over itself like hands fastening
and unfastening what they couldn't secure.

To the Reader

The marker reads DIED FIGHT, a revision
chanced by wind and sand allied

on the nearby shore, *i, n* and *g* visible
only to those—knees thrust into scraggly grass—

who bend studiously, fingers tracing
faint tracks once grooved deeply, quickly,

by a man who never knew the dead man's name,
but whose hands halved and quartered

and blocked into rough-hewn impermanence
this wooden cross, a last but not

lasting record of a life renamed, then named again
as a breaking of time's back.

Or as a moment poised to split into halves—after,
before—along an imperceptible fracture

that doesn't yet crack. What do you hope for, love,
bent there like a scholar to her book?

To resolve nearly scoured-away shapes
into sound, to voice some other, weathered voice,

to wrench sequence and syntax back into line
against the shore-wind's daily craft?

How poor to die the anonymous, unwritten
subject of one's own death, to be known

only as a fading final act in a sentence
constantly ground into fragment, particle.

Or perhaps I've read too much into things,
watching from the bluff above the bay.

Over here! Look up! And now I see what's caught
your eye. A sheath of sand scours past

but still you can't rub it from your sight.

The Poet's House

Through one window the dim light of a crook-necked lamp
presides over a pencil sharpened to a fresh point
and a sheaf of paper scrawled with dust

but not one word the poet ever wrote. It is as if
someone has stepped away, into another room,
beyond view, beyond what remains—always now—

unimagined. Still, to see it, the hint of a hand
in the tidiness of the stack, and in the books
shadowed on a shelf like houses doused for the night

in a city of the famous and not quite forgotten
where along narrow streets you can just make out plaques
adorning the residences: Moore, Herbert—Zbigniew

and George—Baudelaire, Finch and Swift.
Around one corner Keats's cat prowls—the same one,
slight and black, that sprawled your lap at his grave—

then, tired of her hunt, settles by a door to clean herself
through the hours until dawn. But outside this window,
just the plain planked facing of a single house, unmarked,

unnamed. To find it you must cross an empty field's billowing
lines of snow, beneath a helix of birds, doubled,
tripled in distant undulation and belting a swirl of fray

and repair too dense for any song at all to clear its voice.
A long, bitter walk, but hurry, arrive before the caretaker
who only has at heart keeping you out, who comes

each evening to check no volume has been taken
down, paged through, set aside, to brush away the dust's signature
with a flick of the hand as though flipping a guestbook forward

for the coming day and to douse the lamp for the present night.
She'll cross the same field attended by birdsong
and the first snow falling until it no longer begins

but constantly wisps the air into a rhyme for the sweep
her own blood makes muffled behind scarf-clapped ears.
To clasp the scarf against wind she numbs her hands.

To warm them she loosens the cloth, a long, dark wing
that flutters not as in flight but as a dead thing stirs, black
against snow. Arrive first, kneel beneath the window

as though to collect pages of light cast on the ground.
You'll find, half-buried, stunned, wings askew, lost
from the other singers finally falling mute in darkened trees,

a starling. Watch to see if it will wake, curl its toes
around the absent branch and resume the song half-sung—
always a half and raveled song scored in the blood and breath,

rambled through, wrecked against, bound recklessly to
its other incarnations, the ones in the field today
and all fall and summer, in other years, breaching

generations of throats all the way back and into the poet's living ear.
But you wouldn't come for birdsong, such a common thing
housed everywhere in the world. You hear it in your own yard.

Try the door, then, open it onto the lamplight's hum,
stride past the desk and its empty pages, waiting,
and onto the hush of a street where all the houses stand

within the sound of your voice calling out like a morning bell.

Little Bird

A bird perches on the rail
of the baby's crib, huddles
as though buffeted by wind
and rain. I've seen it, nights,

from the dark corner
of my eye: size of a blackbird
but all grays washed
with a hint of blue.

When I look directly
it flits into a confusion
in the rods and cones,
and I stare until the dark

unfolds, wing by wing,
into nothing but a faint
translucence over the smudge
of her sleeping head.

The bird sings to her in clicks
and squawks when it thinks
no one's listening. I've heard it,
my ear pressed hard to the door—

a song like no song, voice
a hinge, or a chain dragging
the pavement, and the baby's ear
open like a night flower

thrust from the narrow
bed of her unfixed skull.
How can I tell what roots
beneath those tender plates

shifting like thoughts
that can't find a way
to be said? Mornings,
the baby clicks and squawks

when I wake her in a language
she chooses not to speak.

House with a Bed of Tulips

To the photo of her tow-haired father,
three years old and bent nose first
into a profusion of tulips, she said, *No.*
And to the photo of her parents
moving into their first house in a city
she'd never known, *No. Not my home.*
Then, *I want to go inside that picture.*
And that night, after they'd told her
of a time they didn't—couldn't—
yet have her, the daughter dreamed
she found herself below streetlamps
coming to life with a tongue-tied buzz
as though shocked to fill with light
in a neighborhood with its ordinary
little houses—was *every* one painted white?
And this house she paused in front of,
with three squat steps and its rows
of red and gold, this house she could see
inside of when she closed her eyes—
her black dog curled on an orange couch,
her parents crossing paths through the same room—
she knew it wouldn't let her in. No one
would answer her knock. The lock
would grit its teeth against her key. Still,
she stared as though she could stare it open,
and stepped along the walk until something flared
in the window, gauzy, flickering: her reflection
caught there, open-winged, hauling itself
back from what it couldn't pass
so easily through. *Why didn't you let me in?*
she asks when we come to her bed,
then wants a last book before the night's
last hours slip past and she wakes
in her only home. But this is not a story
in which want always has its way. She can't be read
back into another life, to fill a lack
that for a time was all that called us home.

At Seven

One path through the woods leads to these crazed
dispatches of red-veined, face-sized leaves. I pick up a leaf,

cover my eyes and no one recognizes me, no one can see me,
no one knows I'm here; even the river misses my face

fallen on its wake, and slips under, tarnished, pictureless,
wrecked with light. Not a surprise. When I was born,

there was a commotion outside. *Is it me?* I thought,
or something like it—this, before there were words

—but Father went to the window and looked out
on whatever arrived or departed unexpectedly.

Then I lost track; Mother whispered a song in my ear,
and something filled my mouth. It was like that for a while.

When there were words, so many came I didn't know
which to try; my tongue swelled at each, bee-stung,

harried by rash and rasp: Ma, Da, bye and bird,
and word for what I cannot touch. I'll tell you

what childhood was like: medicine that tasted like berries.
And how they made me sit in the same tree, every year,

rough bark on the backs of my legs. Once something flew
out of the branches—scissortail, boat-tail, waxwing, kite—

names, names, but none wanted to be there with me.
Each year was vast as another country, a confusion at the borders,

a new slate of customs to be learned. Easy to forget
what you're not supposed to do. Easy, too, to do it.

Once, in a square we crossed, a woman threw her hands
up and pigeons rained down. They crawled

over each other, a ball of wings churning the cobbles.
When I called to them, the air thrummed, it was like being

inside their wings, inside *flying*, all whisper and rush . . .
And they didn't want to leave, settling at my feet, but still

the woman *hissed* at me. Makes you wonder what
you've missed. What did Father watch from the window?

When he turned back he was changed—*dour* is one of Mother's
words for it. And Mother, I've forgotten even the sound

of what she sang . . . The river's static turns up high,
scrub-a-dub-dub, and I'm lost again, here where a trunk

has toppled over the water, last night's snow across its back
trailed through by sure-footing I can't follow to the other bank

and its unfamiliar trees. Something knew where it was going,
some creature I've never seen, and perhaps it's never seen

the likes of me, either, and turns, out of sight
in the slatted dark, to look back at the new. And hisses.

Miguel Hernández, Madrid, 1934

Before his father turned back from the news to tend
the goats' predictable appetites in the stony yard,

before the exiled breath hissed from Miguel's teeth
in the last of his prisons, before even the first water

ached his lungs and the one long needle's pierce
and pull spread air deeply in his chest again,

before the photograph of his own son burst into wings
under the warden's hand, wafted skyward, tinsel and ash,

before his wife suckled their son, little lark, on whatever
milk her body could dredge from its meal of onions,

before the late poems led to a last, and everything
asked of him was given, or given up,

Miguel clambered into a tree's branches arched over
a bustled city street to sing for another poet,

poor man, who'd only heard a nightingale's song
in poems, in words, in the tink and hollow plunk

of syllables tossed in a pauper's cup; climbed
—Madrid below him tilted as if reeling,

its many eyes snapped back and staring up—
to breathe in the city falling silent, the city

that would fall, given time, to the army rooting
through the provinces, but not now, not this moment

pocketed in his lungs, a private currency
stamped with the inverted sprawl of wings

his lips purse to pay out as wordless song—

After the Shipwreck

We come down to the lake, a habit as rote
and written into our muscles these summer evenings
as the waves scribbling their alphabet

across the water. Tonight, the lake
has made arrangements for us, returning
what was never ours: a beam prized from a shipwreck

down the shore. All that traveling toward us
so perfectly timed. We drag it higher on the beach,
then settle to watch the waves rush a broken cursive of Cs.

I'm a student of such matters, what comes
in waves, in foam and clatter, curl and scuffle,
what's found and lost and shuffled

by each melancholy roller ridden
with its idiosyncrasies of light. The lake
changes within its limits, I change within mine;

I take no joy in this. But in this:
a freighter passes at the horizon, lit already
for its travel through the dark. And then it is darker.

The night I've felt coming for hours reaches
its palm over your shoulder to brush the lake clean,
though for now you'll stay here with me, won't you, love.

Fire & Tulips

1.

When my wife described pushing open the unlocked
front door her family had left through for good
when she was six, and walking into the house
where now strangers slept, a new family

of night sounds ticking like hour hands in their beds,
I imagined she entered the door I found in a photo
rifled from a bin of second-hand portraits—
anonymous, battered, fifteen cents apiece.

I'd bought the picture for the year of her birth bleared
in ink on the backside, for the front glazed
and crackled like a vessel wrecked in a kiln's blast;
for how this photo of a small white house

and its bed of tulips couldn't hold the story
it was meant to hold: *whose* house, *whose* hands set bulbs
so precisely to break in rows like orderly fires
along the wall. How the photo left among its losses

room for something new: a whole minor history
spills through, sweeping the steps clean
on its way out the door . . . And when she said,
The dream again, hand to her belly's restless,

late-come shuffle, I imagined even we were swept
clean of the years when no matter how often
and in how many ways we asked more of them,
our bodies made nothing but pleasure and waste.

*

Houses won't hold us;

> *they frame us*
> *as we flare—*

same breeze
that moments

ago tucked
us in.

2.

A door slammed; someone went out, or did
someone come back in? Still, third night
in a row a noise roused her from her childhood
bed in the strangers' home, from the pillow

with her name hand-stitched at the hem
and crowded with the bright, imprecise
outlines of flowers in the room in the house
my wife found she couldn't stay out of,

where, as a child she dreamed a whole
other life than the one she's bound to now.
A pregnancy dream, she called it, this return
to childhood common as nausea,

return to a house beyond the outskirts
of our life together, a far settlement
where streetlights burn through the distance,
dead as stars. And I see her standing

where someone else once paused on a sidewalk
to snap a photo of the last moment a house
could be taken as her own, before strangers
woke like matches from their beds . . .

I saw her as a shadow cast into the photo,
out of our lives and into her own. I couldn't imagine
how all that longing, built and razed and come
at last to what we wanted, could lead her here.

*

What do they

           want, these empty faces

        from any past

           but our own? The door

                is open—

3.

Weeks and the tulips fell apart, not meant
to last, reds and golds broken-backed
and wasted to browns, disjointed stalks thrust
from the ground. But when the photo arrived

in a packet of other photos, it was flush
with those colors again, though smaller, contained
now, preserved. One photo out of how many
thumbed through once or twice, set aside . . .

And then—*when* did it happen?—the only photo
I found like it in the bin veined everywhere with heat
as though someone had tossed the image
at a rising flame and meant to be done with it,

all of it: photo, house, tidy bed of tulips,
the whole province of home and family,
tiers of flame sweeping back through the rafters
of a private, inscrutable history of ache or rage

or irretrievable joy . . . But the picture
didn't catch, didn't burn to ash and negative.
The heat toyed with it, scrawled a few remarks,
then left it for someone else to find, to save,

to box away as though the scene still held a flicker
of meaning . . . Until it didn't, and someone else
sold the photo with a stack of other photos
outlasting any memory anyone would want to claim.

*

Touch it with a match—

       a red-

              rimmed crack will open

           the paper backing,

                 a false horizon,

           a yawning

                and bewildered

                               smile.

4.

And now this photo of a young woman and man
stepping out to the front steps of a house—
or are they on their way back in?—how
unexceptional they look. Already something's

been tidied up, swept away behind the glances
they steady at the camera. One moment of light
sifted out of three years, each month
fire-swept, splintered into cinder and ash,

a fine soot coating their tongues
as they trailed through the same rooms,
this couple who couldn't make a child
on their own, each month's needles

driven home to no point, to no end
they'd wanted, punctuating day after day
with the paraphernalia of their failure,
of their treatment, whichever, it was hard then

to see a difference . . . Until it was over,
and they found themselves in another house
waiting for a face to put a name to . . . Still,
I can't say they ever thought it would end,

this new house no different from the old:
they've tried again to make the one thing
they find again they can't. How can they want
to go back in, how can they go anywhere else?

*

Lights flare. A door

                grazes

                      its frame. Someone's

                coming, someone's coming

                        through the doorway,

                    head made

                      of a distant

                        blazing . . .

5.

Will someone want us, rifling the cast-offs
in the bin, photos of the long dead, the anonymous,
and lift to the light our faces clear and empty
as a glass held to a tap? How thirsty

she must be, to call the breathless out of blankness
and into the foreign element of now, the way,
half-awake, lost between lives, your mother
roused last night from some new dream

to bring you the glass of water you called for;
she paused over the shadow-pooled sink
as though she couldn't remember where glasses
were kept, or even which house she was in.

So I claim this constellation of photos
cast across my desk for you: this one of a child
forged pixel by pixel from your parents' faces
the first time we imagined a daughter,

five dollars in a novelty photo booth.
She came as the worst sum of our features:
crooked nose, crooked mouth, face
made of halves, of miscalculation

and the mechanical force of will
we didn't yet know we'd need. And this one
of me as a child, standing in the wooded yard
of a home you'll never see. A dog runs

past the frame, already halfway gone,
as I lean on my father's battered truck
that must be a shell of rust by now
if it survives at all, brittle, mottled in orange

and ochre like a slow and heatless fire
that smolders—exactly unlike memory—
with a mindless purpose to undo what
it never knew how to make in the first place.

And I claim with a quick trace of ink this photo
of you tipped back in your mother's arms as though
laughter pours from your body where we pose
before a sprawling pen at an animal preserve

in a Midwestern woods, the shape rearing
behind us out of focus, unrecognizable
as anything but a darkness rimmed with light
burning to consume us with what I now call joy.

Acknowledgments

Many of the poems in this book appeared in the following journals:

Cincinnati Review: "House with a Bed of Tulips"

Harvard Review: "The String"

New England Review: "Three Bridges," "Sleeper Lake Fire,"
    "After the Shipwreck"

New Writing: "Little Bird," "Bell"

Pleiades: "The Black Bear at Closing"

Ploughshares: "Semper Augustus"

Poetry Daily: "Dumb Luck"

Poetry Northwest: "And Winter"

POOL: "Lullaby"

Seattle Review: "A Brief Account of My Thirty-Third Year"

Southwest Review: "At Seven"

Subtropics: "Loss"

Third Coast: "Fire & Tulips"

The Threepenny Review: "Dumb Luck," "The Radio Tree"

TriQuarterly: "Hotel Fire," "The Empty Theater," "The Lake,"
    "The Poet's House," "To the Reader"

Virginia Quarterly Review: "Miguel Hernández, Madrid, 1934"

"Three Bridges" appeared in *Legitimate Dangers: American Poets of the New Century*, edited by Cate Marvin and Michael Dumanis (Sarabande Books, 2005).

"The Poet's House" appeared in *Poetry 30: Thirtysomething American Thirtysomething Poets*, edited by Gerry LaFemina (Mammoth Books, 2005).

The National Endowment for the Arts and the University of North Texas provided me with invaluable support during the writing of this collection. I am grateful to Christopher Bakken, Bruce Bond, Andrew Feld, Greg Fraser, Edward Hirsch, Alan Michael Parker, and Pimone Triplett for their keen insights that helped guide this book, as well as to New Issues Press and my editor, William Olsen, for their hard and good work. I'm also thankful for the encouragement and patience of my family and friends, especially Lea Marks, Jacque Vanhoutte and Alex Pettit. And above all, I'm indebted to Amy Taylor, whose love and confidence have carried me through.

photo by Amy Taylor

Corey Marks' *Renunciation* was a National Poetry Series selection.
His poems have appeared in *New England Review*, *The Paris Review*,
Ploughshares, *The Threepenny Review*, and *TriQuarterly*. He has
received a fellowship from the National Endowment for the Arts,
the Natalie Ornish Prize from the Texas Institute of Letters, and the
Bernard F. Conners Prize from *The Paris Review*. He teaches at the
University of North Texas.

The Green Rose Prize

2011: Corey Marks
The Radio Tree

2010: Seth Abramson
Northerners

2009: Malinda Markham
Having Cut the Sparrow's Heart

2008: Patty Seyburn
Hilarity

2007: Jon Pineda
The Translator's Diary

2006: Noah Eli Gordon
A Fiddle Pulled from the Throat of a Sparrow

2005: Joan Houlihan
The Mending Worm

2004: Hugh Seidman
Somebody Stand Up and Sing

2003: Christine Hume
Alaskaphrenia
Gretchen Mattox
Buddha Box

2002: Christopher Bursk
Ovid at Fifteen

2001: Ruth Ellen Kocher
When the Moon Knows You're Wandering

2000: Martha Rhodes
Perfect Disappearance